The Joyful Path: Finding Happiness Through Self-Discovery

Rizwan Raheem Ahmed, Ph.D.

DEDICATION

This book is dedicated to my Late Mother and Father who have provided me the financial, emotional, and Parental opportunities to raise me, provided higher education and supported me in my initial professional life journey.

TABLE OF CONTENTS

ACKNOWLEDGMENTS

I Acknowledge my wife who has supported me during writing this book. She has also helped me to generate book cover and other relevant material on Photoshop. She has encouraged me all the way in my journey.

INTRODUCTION

Background on the concept of happiness

The pursuit of happiness is a universal goal that transcends all cultures and societies. Despite the diversity in human experience, we all share a common desire to find joy and fulfillment in our lives. Happiness is not a new concept. Philosophers, scientists, and spiritual leaders have explored and studied the nature of happiness for centuries. From Aristotle to the Dalai Lama, there is a wealth of knowledge and wisdom on the subject.

Happiness is a complex and multifaceted concept that can be understood from different perspectives. Some define happiness as a feeling of pleasure or satisfaction, while others view it as a state of being that arises from living a meaningful and purposeful life. In recent years, researchers have also identified different types of happiness, such as hedonic happiness (pleasure-seeking) and eudaimonic happiness (meaning and fulfillment).

Happiness is not a static state. It is a dynamic process that involves a combination of factors, including genetics, environment, and personal choices. While some people may have a genetic predisposition to happiness, research suggests that environmental factors, such as social support, positive relationships, and healthy lifestyle habits, play a significant role in shaping our happiness levels.

Happiness is not only a personal goal but also a societal one. The pursuit of happiness is enshrined in the United States Declaration of Independence, which states that all people have the unalienable right to life, liberty, and the pursuit of happiness. In recent years, there has been a growing interest in happiness at the workplace, in relationships, fitness and wellness, creativity and self-expression, spirituality and mindfulness, financial stability and success, personal growth and development, parenthood and family life, travel and exploration, community involvement, and social activism.

In conclusion, the concept of happiness is a fascinating and complex topic that has captured the attention of people from all walks of life. Whether we are seeking happiness for personal or societal reasons, the pursuit of happiness is a journey that requires self-discovery, mindfulness, and intentional living. The Joyful Path offers insights and tools to help readers embark on this journey and discover their unique path to happiness.

Overview of Self-discovery as a Means to Find Happiness

Self-discovery is a journey that can lead to a greater understanding of oneself and the world around us. It is a process of becoming aware of one's thoughts, feelings, and behaviors and using that awareness to make positive changes in one's life. Self-discovery can be a powerful tool for finding happiness, as it enables individuals to identify their passions, values, and goals, and to align their lives with those things.

Happiness is a subjective experience, and what brings joy and fulfillment to one person may not be the same for another. However, self-discovery can help individuals identify what brings them happiness and allow them to pursue those things. It can also help individuals identify and work through any negative thought patterns or limiting beliefs that may be holding them back from experiencing happiness.

In the workplace, self-discovery can lead to greater job satisfaction and fulfillment. By identifying one's strengths and passions, individuals can find careers that align with their values and bring them joy. Additionally, self-discovery can help individuals navigate workplace relationships and conflicts more effectively, leading to a more positive work environment.

In relationships, self-discovery can help individuals identify their needs and communicate them effectively to their partners. By understanding their own emotions and behaviors, individuals can also develop greater empathy and understanding towards their partners, leading to more fulfilling relationships.

Self-discovery can also be a powerful tool for enhancing fitness and wellness. By understanding one's motivations and barriers to exercise and healthy habits, individuals can develop strategies to overcome those barriers and achieve greater physical and mental well-being.

For those interested in creativity and self-expression, self-discovery can help individuals identify their unique talents and passions and find ways to express them. This can lead to greater fulfillment and a sense of purpose in life.

Spirituality and mindfulness can also be avenues for self-discovery. By exploring one's beliefs and values, individuals can find greater meaning and purpose in life. Mindfulness practices, such as meditation, can also help individuals develop greater self-awareness and a greater sense of inner peace.

Financial stability and success can also be a source of happiness, and self-discovery can help individuals identify their financial goals and develop strategies for achieving them. By understanding their values and priorities, individuals can also make more intentional decisions about money and find greater fulfillment in their financial lives.

Personal growth and development are also key aspects of self-discovery. By identifying areas for growth and development, individuals can take steps to improve themselves and their lives. This can lead to greater fulfillment and a sense of accomplishment.

In parenthood and family life, self-discovery can help individuals identify their parenting styles and develop strategies for raising happy and healthy children. By understanding their values and priorities, individuals can also create more harmonious family dynamics.

For those interested in travel and exploration, self-discovery can help individuals identify their travel goals and find ways to experience new cultures and environments that align with their values and interests. This can lead to greater fulfillment and a sense of adventure.

Finally, self-discovery can be a powerful tool for community involvement and social activism. By understanding one's values and priorities, individuals can identify causes they are passionate about and find ways to make a difference in their communities and the world.

Overall, self-discovery is a powerful means to find happiness in all areas of life. By becoming more self-aware and aligning one's life with one's values and passions, individuals can find greater fulfillment and joy.

CHAPTER 1: UNDERSTANDING HAPPINESS

Defining happiness and its different types

Happiness is an elusive concept that has been studied by philosophers, psychologists, and scientists for centuries. While there is no universal definition of happiness, it is generally understood as a state of well-being characterized by positive emotions, contentment, and satisfaction with one's life. Happiness is not a fixed state, but rather a dynamic process that evolves and is influenced by a variety of factors.

There are many different types of happiness, each with its unique characteristics and benefits. Some of the most common types of happiness include:

1. Hedonic happiness: This type of happiness is based on pleasure and the pursuit of positive experiences. It is associated with short-term gratification and the pursuit of pleasure and enjoyment.

2. Eudaimonic happiness: This type of happiness is based on a sense of purpose and meaning in life. It is associated with long-term fulfillment and the pursuit of personal growth and self-improvement.

3. Social happiness: This type of happiness is based on social connections and relationships. It is associated with a sense of belonging and community and the pursuit of social support and connection.

4. Spiritual happiness: This type of happiness is based on spiritual or religious beliefs. It is associated with a sense of purpose and meaning in life and the pursuit of spiritual growth and enlightenment.

5. Intellectual happiness: This type of happiness is based on the pursuit of knowledge and intellectual stimulation. It is associated with the pursuit of intellectual challenges and the fulfillment that comes from learning and exploring new ideas.

6. Physical happiness: This type of happiness is based on physical health and wellness. It is associated with the pursuit of physical fitness, healthy eating, and self-care.

Understanding the different types of happiness can help you identify what brings you joy and fulfillment in life. By focusing on the types of happiness that are most important to you, you can develop a plan for achieving greater happiness and well-being in your life. Whether it is through pursuing personal growth, cultivating social connections, or finding meaning and purpose in your work, many paths to happiness can help you live a more joyful and fulfilling life.

The impact of happiness on mental and physical health

The impact of happiness on mental and physical health is a topic that has been extensively researched and studied over the years. It is no secret that happiness and well-being are closely linked. Happy people tend to be healthier both mentally and physically. Happiness is often associated with a positive outlook on life, which can lead to better coping mechanisms and resilience in the face of adversity.

Mentally, happiness has been shown to reduce the risk of depression, anxiety, and stress. It also improves cognitive functioning, memory, and decision-making abilities. Happy people tend to have better relationships with others, which can lead to a sense of belonging and social connectedness.

Physically, happiness has been linked to a lower risk of developing chronic diseases such as heart disease, stroke, and diabetes. It also boosts the immune system, reduces inflammation and pain, and leads to better sleep.

Happiness in the workplace is especially important. Happy employees tend to be more productive, creative and engaged. They are also more likely to stay with their current employer and have better relationships with their co-workers. Employers who prioritize employee happiness often see a return on investment through increased profits and reduced turnover rates.

Happiness in relationships is also crucial. Couples who are happy tend to have better communication, more intimacy, and less conflict. They also tend to be more supportive of each other, which can lead to a greater sense of emotional security and stability.

Happiness through fitness and wellness is another area where the benefits are clear. People who exercise regularly and eat a healthy diet tend to be happier and more satisfied with their lives. Exercise releases endorphins, which are natural mood boosters. It also helps to reduce stress and anxiety.

Happiness through creativity and self-expression is also important. Engaging in creative activities such as painting, writing, or music can be a form of therapy that helps to reduce stress and anxiety. It also provides a sense of accomplishment and fulfillment.

Happiness through spirituality and mindfulness is becoming increasingly popular. Practices such as meditation and yoga have been shown to reduce stress, improve mental health, and increase feelings of well-being. They also provide a sense of purpose and meaning in life.

Happiness through financial stability and success is also important. People who feel financially secure tend to be happier and less stressed. They also have greater freedom to pursue their passions and interests.

Happiness through personal growth and development is a lifelong journey. People who are open to learning and growing tend to be happier and more fulfilled. They also tend to have better relationships and a greater sense of purpose in life.

Happiness in parenthood and family life is another area where the benefits are clear. Happy parents tend to have happier children. They also tend to be more patient, loving, and nurturing.

Happiness in travel and exploration is another way to find joy in life. Travel allows people to experience new cultures, meet new people, and create lasting memories. It also provides an opportunity to step outside of one's comfort zone and challenge oneself.

Happiness through community involvement and social activism is another way to find fulfillment. Volunteering, activism, and community service provide a sense of purpose and meaning in life. They also allow people to make a positive impact on the world around them.

In conclusion, happiness is a vital component of overall well-being. The benefits of happiness are numerous and far-reaching, impacting every aspect of life. By prioritizing happiness and making positive changes in our lives, we can experience greater joy, fulfillment, and success.

The role of genetics and environment in happiness

Happiness is often considered an elusive concept, but

research has shown that it can be influenced by both genetic and environmental factors. It is estimated that genetics account for about 50% of our happiness level, while the remaining 50% is influenced by our environment and personal choices.

Genetics plays a significant role in our happiness level. Studies have shown that some people are naturally predisposed to be happy, while others may have a genetic disposition towards depression or anxiety. However, genetics do not determine our happiness level entirely. Environmental factors and personal choices can also affect our happiness level.

Environment plays an essential role in our happiness level. Our surroundings, including our relationships, work environment, and physical environment, can have a significant impact on our happiness. For example, people who live in areas with high levels of pollution, crime, or noise tend to have lower levels of happiness than those living in more peaceful and clean environments.

Personal choices also play a vital role in our happiness level. Choices such as engaging in physical activity, practicing mindfulness and spirituality, pursuing creative interests, and community involvement can significantly impact our happiness. Financial stability and success can also contribute to our happiness level, but the correlation is not as strong as one might think.

In conclusion, while genetics play a significant role in our happiness level, environmental factors, and personal choices are equally important. It is essential to understand that happiness is not a destination but a journey, and we can take steps to increase our happiness level by making conscious choices and surrounding ourselves with positivity, love, and joy. The key to finding happiness lies in self-discovery, which involves understanding our unique selves, values, and purpose in life.

CHAPTER 2: HAPPINESS IN THE WORKPLACE

The benefits of happiness in the workplace

The benefits of happiness in the workplace cannot be overemphasized. A happy workplace is a productive one, and this is because happiness is a natural motivator. When employees are happy, they are more likely to be engaged, committed, and passionate about their work. They take pride in what they do, and this translates to better performance, improved customer satisfaction, and increased profitability.

Research has shown that happy employees are more creative, innovative, and collaborative. They are more likely to share ideas and work together to solve problems, leading to better decision-making and improved problem-solving skills. Happy employees are also more resilient and adaptable, making them better equipped to handle change and uncertainty.

Furthermore, a happy workplace fosters positive relationships among employees. This leads to a sense of belonging and camaraderie, which in turn reduces stress and burnout. Happy employees are also less likely to engage in negative behaviors such as absenteeism, turnover, and conflict.

In addition to the benefits to the organization, happy employees also experience personal benefits. They are more likely to have a better work-life balance, leading to improved mental and physical health. They are also more likely to enjoy greater job satisfaction, which can lead to career advancement and increased earning potential.

Overall, the benefits of happiness in the workplace cannot be overstated. Organizations that prioritize employee happiness are more likely to attract and retain top talent, increase productivity and profitability, and foster a positive work environment. As an individual, prioritizing your happiness in the workplace can lead to personal and professional growth, improved well-being, and a fulfilling career.

Strategies for finding happiness at work

Work is an essential part of life, and it should not only be a means of earning a living but also a source of joy and fulfillment. Finding happiness at work is crucial to our overall well-being, and it can significantly impact our relationships, personal growth, and financial success. Here are some strategies for finding happiness at work.

1. Pursue your passion: One of the best ways to find happiness at work is to do something that you are passionate about. When you are doing something that you love, it becomes more than just a job, and you feel a sense of purpose and fulfillment.

2. Cultivate positive relationships: Positive relationships with coworkers and managers can significantly impact your happiness at work. Surround yourself with people who inspire you, support you, and make you feel good about yourself.

3. Practice gratitude: Focusing on the positive aspects of your job and being grateful for the opportunities it offers can help you find happiness at work. Take time to appreciate the things you enjoy about your job, whether it's the people you work with, the work itself, or the benefits you receive.

4. Set realistic goals: Setting achievable goals can give you a sense of purpose and direction at work. It can also help you feel more satisfied and motivated when you accomplish them.

5. Take breaks: Taking regular breaks can help you maintain your energy and focus throughout the day. Whether it's a short walk, a cup of tea, or a quick chat with a colleague, taking breaks can help you recharge and feel more refreshed.

6. Learn new skills: Learning new skills can help you feel more engaged and challenged at work. It can also open up new opportunities for growth and advancement.

7. Practice mindfulness: Mindfulness can help you stay present and focused at work, even during stressful or challenging situations. Taking a few moments to breathe deeply, meditate, or practice mindfulness exercises can help you feel calmer and centered.

In conclusion, finding happiness at work is possible, and it requires intentional effort and a positive attitude. By pursuing your passion, cultivating positive relationships, practicing gratitude, setting realistic goals, taking breaks, learning new skills, and practicing mindfulness, you can find joy and fulfillment in your work and improve your overall well-being.

The impact of work-life balance on happiness

The impact of work-life balance on happiness is a crucial aspect of living a joyful life. When we spend most of our time working, it can lead to feelings of burnout, exhaustion, and stress, ultimately affecting our mental and physical health. It is essential to strike a balance between work and personal life to achieve a life filled with happiness and contentment.

When we prioritize our personal lives, it allows us to engage in activities that make us happy, such as spending time with loved ones, pursuing hobbies, and exploring new experiences. This, in turn, helps to boost our mood, reduce stress, and increase overall life satisfaction. By prioritizing our personal life, we can also improve our relationships with family, friends, and loved ones, leading to a more fulfilling life.

On the other hand, when we focus solely on our work life, it can lead to feelings of isolation, disconnection, and loneliness. It can also lead to negative impacts on our relationships, affecting our ability to connect with our loved ones and creating a sense of distance between us.

Furthermore, work-life balance is also essential for maintaining physical health. When we are overworked, we may neglect our physical health, leading to problems such as lack of sleep, poor diet, and lack of exercise. These issues can ultimately lead to long-term health problems that can affect our happiness and well-being.

In conclusion, work-life balance is a crucial aspect of achieving happiness and contentment in life. It is essential to prioritize personal life, maintain relationships, and take care of our physical health. By doing so, we can live a life filled with joy, positivity, and fulfillment.

CHAPTER 3: HAPPINESS IN RELATIONSHIPS

The importance of healthy relationships for happiness

The importance of healthy relationships for happiness cannot be overstated. Humans are social creatures, and we thrive when we have strong connections with others. Whether it's with our family members, friends, romantic partners, or colleagues, having healthy relationships can greatly contribute to our overall happiness and well-being.

Healthy relationships are characterized by mutual respect, trust, honesty, and open communication. When we have these qualities in our relationships, we feel safe, supported, and valued. We can be our authentic selves and share our thoughts and feelings without fear of judgment or rejection.

In contrast, unhealthy relationships can be toxic and

draining. They may involve manipulation, control, or abuse, and can leave us feeling isolated, anxious, or depressed. It's important to recognize the signs of an unhealthy relationship and take steps to address them, whether it's through setting boundaries, seeking counselling, or ending the relationship altogether.

At work, having positive relationships with colleagues can lead to greater job satisfaction and productivity. When we feel respected and valued by our co-workers, we're more likely to enjoy our work and feel motivated to do our best. Similarly, having supportive friends and family members can provide a sense of belonging and help us navigate life's challenges.

Maintaining healthy relationships requires effort and commitment. It means being willing to listen, compromise, and forgive. It also means being honest about our needs and boundaries and respecting those of others. When we invest in our relationships, we reap the rewards of greater happiness and fulfillment in our lives.

In addition to interpersonal relationships, it's also important to cultivate a healthy relationship with ourselves. This means practicing self-care, setting healthy boundaries, and treating ourselves with kindness and compassion. When we have a positive self-image and a strong sense of self-worth, we're more likely to attract healthy relationships into our lives.

Overall, healthy relationships are essential for happiness and well-being. Whether it's through our personal, professional, or community connections, investing in our relationships can bring us greater joy and fulfillment in all areas of our lives.

Strategies for Building and Maintaining Happy Relationships

Humans are social beings, and we thrive on healthy relationships. However, building and maintaining happy relationships can be a daunting task, especially in today's fast-paced world. It takes effort, patience, and self-awareness to create meaningful connections with others. In this chapter, we will explore some strategies for building and maintaining happy relationships.

1. Communication: Communication is the foundation of any healthy relationship. It is essential to communicate your thoughts and feelings honestly and openly with your partner. Listen to your partner's concerns and empathize with them. Avoid criticizing or blaming them and instead offer constructive feedback.

2. Empathy: Empathy is the ability to understand and share the feelings of another person. It is crucial in building and maintaining a happy relationship. Try to put yourself in your partner's shoes and understand their perspective. This will help you develop a deeper connection with them.

3. Respect: Respect is an essential component of any healthy relationship. It is essential to respect your partner's boundaries, opinions, and decisions. Avoid belittling or demeaning them, and instead, celebrate their achievements and support their goals.

4. Quality time: Spending quality time together is crucial in building a happy relationship. Engage in activities that you both enjoy and make time for each other regularly. This will help you bond and create lasting memories.

5. Forgiveness: No relationship is perfect, and conflicts are bound to arise. It is essential to forgive your partner and move forward. Holding onto grudges or resentment can damage the relationship.

6. Personal growth: Personal growth and development are crucial in building and maintaining happy relationships. Work on improving yourself, and encourage your partner to do the same. This will help you both grow individually and together.

In conclusion, building and maintaining happy relationships requires effort, patience, and self-awareness. By practicing effective communication, empathy, respect, spending quality time together, forgiveness, and personal growth, you can create meaningful connections with others. Remember, a happy relationship is a two-way street, and it takes the effort of both partners to make it work.

The impact of communication and empathy on happiness in relationships

The impact of communication and empathy on happiness in relationships cannot be overstated. Communication is the foundation of any relationship, and without it, there can be no meaningful connection. Empathy, on the other hand, is the ability to understand and share the feelings of another person. When these two elements are present in a relationship, happiness is sure to follow.

Communication is key to any successful relationship. It allows us to express our thoughts and feelings, share our hopes and dreams, and work through any issues that may arise. When we communicate effectively, we build trust and understanding with our partners. This, in turn, leads to deeper intimacy and a stronger connection.

Empathy is equally important in a relationship. It allows us to put ourselves in our partner's shoes and understand their perspective. When we show empathy, we demonstrate that we care about our partner's feelings and are willing to work through any challenges together. This can create a sense of safety and security in the relationship, which can lead to greater happiness and fulfillment.

When communication and empathy are lacking in a relationship, the opposite is true. Misunderstandings can occur, trust can be broken, and feelings of isolation and loneliness can set in. These negative emotions can lead to unhappiness and even the breakdown of the relationship.

If you want to cultivate happiness in your relationships, make communication and empathy a priority. Take the time to listen to your partner, express your own thoughts and feelings, and work together to find solutions to any challenges that arise. Show empathy by putting yourself in your partner's shoes and understanding their perspective. By doing so, you can create a strong, healthy relationship that brings joy and fulfillment to both of you.

CHAPTER 4: HAPPINESS THROUGH FITNESS AND WELLNESS

The connection between physical health and happiness

The connection between physical health and happiness is undeniable. When we take care of our bodies, we feel better both physically and mentally. Exercise, healthy eating, and regular check-ups with healthcare professionals are all important components of physical health.

But why does physical health impact our happiness? There are a few reasons. First, exercise releases endorphins, which are chemicals in the brain that make us feel good. This is often referred to as a "runner's high." Second, when we take care of our bodies, we feel better about ourselves. We have more confidence and self-esteem, which can lead to a more positive outlook on life. Finally, physical health can reduce stress and anxiety, which are major contributors to unhappiness.

In the workplace, physical health is important for a few reasons. First, healthy employees are less likely to miss work due to illness. This means that companies with healthy employees have higher productivity and lower healthcare costs. Additionally, physically healthy employees are often happier and more engaged in their work.

In relationships, physical health can also play a role. When we feel good about ourselves, we are more likely to attract positive relationships. Additionally, couples who exercise together often report feeling closer and more connected.

Fitness and wellness are obvious contributors to physical health and happiness. Regular exercise and a healthy diet can improve both physical and mental health. Additionally, activities like yoga and meditation can reduce stress and promote relaxation.

Creativity and self-expression are also important factors in happiness. Activities like painting, writing, or playing music can be therapeutic and promote a sense of well-being. Additionally, these activities can help us express ourselves and connect with others who share our interests.

Spirituality and mindfulness can also promote happiness. Practices like meditation and prayer can help us connect with something greater than ourselves and find meaning in life. Additionally, these practices can help us find inner peace and reduce stress and anxiety.

Financial stability and success are often seen as contributors to happiness. However, it's important to note that money alone does not bring happiness. Financial stability can provide a sense of security and reduce stress, but it's important to also focus on other areas of life that contribute to happiness.

Personal growth and development are important for overall happiness. When we set goals and work towards them, we feel a sense of accomplishment and purpose. Additionally, learning new skills and trying new things can be exciting and promote personal growth.

In parenthood and family life, physical health is important for setting a good example for children. Additionally, being healthy allows us to be more present and engaged with our families.

Travel and exploration can also promote happiness. Seeing new places and experiencing new things can be exciting and broaden our perspectives.

Finally, community involvement and social activism can promote happiness by allowing us to connect with others and make a positive impact on the world. When we feel like we are making a difference, we are more likely to feel fulfilled and happy.

Overall, physical health is a key component of happiness. By taking care of our bodies, we can improve both our physical and mental health and lead happier, more fulfilling lives.

Strategies for incorporating fitness and wellness into daily life

Incorporating fitness and wellness into our daily lives can be a challenge, especially with busy schedules and endless distractions. However, making these practices a priority is essential to creating a happier and healthier life.

One strategy for incorporating fitness and wellness into daily life is to make it a part of your routine. This means scheduling time for exercise or meditation just like you would schedule a meeting or appointment. By making it a non-negotiable part of your day, you are more likely to stick to it and make it a habit.

Another strategy is to find activities that you enjoy. Exercise doesn't have to be boring or repetitive. Try different types of workouts or classes until you find something that you truly enjoy. You can also incorporate physical activity into everyday tasks, such as taking the stairs instead of the elevator or walking or biking to work instead of driving.

Mindfulness and meditation are also important components of overall wellness. By taking a few minutes each day to quiet your mind and focus on your breath, you can reduce stress and anxiety, improve concentration, and increase feelings of calm and contentment.

In addition to physical and mental wellness, it's important to focus on nutrition and self-care. Eating a balanced diet with plenty of fruits, vegetables, and whole grains can improve energy levels and overall health. Taking time for self-care activities, such as getting enough sleep, practicing relaxation techniques, and indulging in hobbies or interests, can also contribute to feelings of happiness and well-being.

Finally, it's important to remember that wellness is a journey and not a destination. Don't become discouraged if you miss a workout or indulge in an unhealthy meal. Focus on progress, not perfection, and celebrate the small victories along the way.

Incorporating fitness and wellness into your daily life may require some effort and commitment, but the benefits are well worth it. By prioritizing your health and well-being, you can create a happier, more fulfilling life for yourself and those around you.

The impact of mindfulness and self-care on happiness

The impact of mindfulness and self-care on happiness cannot be overemphasized. Mindfulness is the practice of being present in the moment and focusing on your thoughts, feelings, and surroundings without judgment. Self-care is the practice of taking care of yourself physically, emotionally, and mentally. Both practices have been shown to have a significant impact on happiness.

In today's fast-paced world, it is easy to get caught up in the rat race and forget about taking care of yourself. Many people prioritize work and other responsibilities over their well-being. However, neglecting self-care can lead to burnout, stress, and unhappiness. Mindfulness, on the other hand, helps us to slow down and appreciate the present moment. It helps us to be more aware of our thoughts and emotions and to respond to them more positively.

Studies have shown that mindfulness can reduce stress, anxiety, and depression. It can also improve focus, memory, and cognitive function. Practicing mindfulness regularly can lead to a greater sense of well-being and happiness.

Self-care is also essential for happiness. Taking care of yourself physically, emotionally, and mentally can help you feel more energized, positive, and motivated. It can also help you to be more resilient in the face of challenges and setbacks.

Self-care can take many forms, from getting enough sleep and exercise to practicing meditation or taking a relaxing bath. It is important to find activities that work for you and make them a regular part of your routine.

In conclusion, mindfulness and self-care are essential practices for happiness. They help us to be more present, aware, and positive. By making these practices a regular part of our lives, we can cultivate greater happiness, well-being, and fulfillment.

CHAPTER 5: HAPPINESS THROUGH CREATIVITY AND SELF-EXPRESSION

The benefits of creative expression for happiness

Creative expression is a powerful tool that can help individuals achieve happiness in many different areas of their lives. Whether it's through art, music, writing, or any other form of creative expression, the act of creating something can have a profound impact on our overall well-being.

One of the main benefits of creative expression is that it allows us to tap into our emotions and express them healthily and productively. When we create something, we can channel our feelings into a tangible form, which can help us to process and understand them more effectively. This can be particularly helpful for individuals who struggle with anxiety, depression, or other mental health issues.

In addition to its therapeutic benefits, creative expression can also provide a sense of personal fulfillment and accomplishment. When we create something that we are proud of, it can boost our self-esteem and provide a sense of purpose and meaning in our lives. This can be especially important for individuals who feel unfulfilled or dissatisfied in their current jobs or relationships.

Creative expression can also help us to connect with others and build stronger relationships. Whether it's through sharing our work with others or collaborating with others on a creative project, creativity can provide a powerful way to connect with others on a deeper level. This can be particularly helpful for individuals who struggle with social anxiety or who feel disconnected from others.

Finally, creative expression can provide a sense of joy and pleasure that can be hard to find in other areas of our lives. When we create something that we are passionate about, it can provide a sense of joy and fulfillment that can help to counterbalance the stresses and challenges of daily life.

Overall, there are many different benefits to creative expression for happiness. Whether you're looking to improve your mental health, build stronger relationships, or simply find more joy and fulfillment in your life, creativity can be a powerful tool to help you achieve your goals.

Strategies for discovering and cultivating creativity

Creativity is the ability to think outside the box and come up with new and innovative ideas. It is a crucial aspect of happiness in many areas of life, including relationships, the workplace, fitness and wellness, personal growth, and more. However, many people struggle to tap into their creativity and may feel stuck in their routines. Fortunately, several strategies can help you discover and cultivate your creativity.

1. Embrace your curiosity

Curiosity is the driving force behind creativity. When you are curious about something, you are motivated to learn more and explore new ideas. So, if you want to cultivate your creativity, embrace your curiosity. Ask questions, try new things, and be open to new experiences. This will help you expand your horizons and develop new ways of thinking.

2. Practice mindfulness

Mindfulness is the practice of being present in the moment and fully engaged in your surroundings. When you are mindful, you are better able to observe your thoughts and emotions without judgment. This can help you tap into your creativity by allowing you to see things from a new perspective and break out of old patterns of thinking.

3. Engage in creative activities

Engaging in creative activities is a great way to cultivate your creativity. Try writing, painting, dancing, or any other activity that allows you to express yourself creatively. You don't have to be good at it – the point is to have fun and explore your creative side.

4. Collaborate with others

Collaboration is an excellent way to stimulate your creativity. Working with others can help you see things from a new perspective and generate new ideas. Whether it's in the workplace, in a creative project, or in your personal life, collaborating with others can help you cultivate your creativity.

5. Take breaks

Taking breaks is essential for creativity. When you take a break, you give your brain time to rest and recharge. This can help you come up with new ideas and approach problems from a fresh perspective.

In conclusion, cultivating creativity is essential for happiness in many areas of life. By embracing your curiosity, practicing mindfulness, engaging in creative activities, collaborating with others, and taking breaks, you can tap into your creativity and unlock your full potential. So, get out there and start exploring – you never know where your creativity may take you!

CHAPTER 6: HAPPINESS THROUGH SPIRITUALITY AND MINDFULNESS

Strategies for cultivating mindfulness and spiritual practices

Mindfulness and spirituality are essential components of a

happy life. They can help you gain a deeper understanding of yourself, your purpose, and your connection to the world around you. Here are some strategies for cultivating mindfulness and spiritual practices.

1. Start small and be consistent

Mindfulness and spiritual practices are not something you can master overnight. Start small and be consistent. Set aside a few minutes each day for meditation, prayer, or reflection. As you become more comfortable, you can gradually increase the time you spend on these practices.

2. Create a sacred space

Having a dedicated space where you can practice mindfulness and spirituality can help you stay focused and centered. It can be a corner of your room, a garden, or a quiet spot in nature. Decorate it with items that inspire you and make you feel peaceful.

3. Practice gratitude

Gratitude is a powerful tool for cultivating mindfulness and spirituality. Take time each day to reflect on what you are grateful for. Write down three things that you are thankful for each morning or night.

4. Connect with others

Connecting with others who share your spiritual beliefs can be a powerful way to deepen your practice and feel a sense of community. Attend a spiritual retreat, join a meditation group, or volunteer with a local charity.

5. Practice self-care

Taking care of yourself is an essential part of mindfulness and spirituality. Eat a healthy diet, exercise regularly, and get enough sleep. Take time to do things that bring you joy, such as reading, listening to music, or spending time with loved ones.

6. Be present

Mindfulness is about being fully present in the moment. Practice being mindful in your daily activities by focusing on your breath, noticing your surroundings, and being fully engaged in whatever you are doing.

7. Embrace imperfection

Spiritual practices are not about achieving perfection. Embrace your imperfections and be kind to yourself. Remember that mindfulness and spirituality are a journey, not a destination.

In conclusion, cultivating mindfulness and spiritual practices can help you find happiness, purpose, and fulfillment in your life. By starting small, being consistent, and embracing imperfection, you can deepen your practice and experience the many benefits of mindfulness and spirituality.

The impact of mindfulness on stress reduction and happiness

The impact of mindfulness on stress reduction and happiness has gained significant attention over the years. Mindfulness is the practice of being present in the moment and accepting it without judgment. It involves paying attention to your thoughts, emotions, and physical sensations with an open and non-reactive attitude.

Stress is a part of life, and it can be caused by various factors such as work, relationships, finances, and health. However, mindfulness has been proven to be an effective tool in managing stress. It helps to reduce the level of cortisol, a stress hormone that is produced by the body. By practicing mindfulness, individuals can learn to regulate their emotions and responses to stress better, enabling them to cope more effectively with challenging situations.

Moreover, mindfulness has a positive impact on happiness. It has been found to increase positive emotions such as joy, gratitude, and contentment. Research has shown that mindfulness practice can lead to changes in brain activity, resulting in increased levels of happiness and well-being.

Incorporating mindfulness into daily activities can be beneficial in many aspects of life. For instance, in the workplace, mindfulness can improve focus, productivity, and overall job satisfaction. Mindfulness practices like meditation and deep breathing can be done during breaks to help employees manage stress and improve their mental health.

In relationships, mindfulness can help individuals communicate more effectively and enhance empathy and compassion towards others. By being present and attentive during conversations, individuals can deepen their connections with their loved ones and improve the quality of their relationships.

Through fitness and wellness, mindfulness can help individuals connect with their bodies and be more aware of their physical sensations. This awareness can lead to better decision-making regarding health and wellness goals, leading to a healthier, happier lifestyle.

In conclusion, mindfulness is a powerful tool that can have a positive impact on stress reduction and happiness. Incorporating mindfulness practices into daily routines can improve various aspects of life, including work, relationships, fitness, and overall well-being.

CHAPTER 7: HAPPINESS THROUGH FINANCIAL STABILITY AND SUCCESS

The connection between money and happiness

Money is often viewed as the key to happiness, but is this

the case? The connection between money and happiness is a complex one, and it's important to understand how they relate to each other.

On one hand, money can provide us with the resources we need to live a comfortable life. It can help us pay for our basic needs like food, shelter, and clothing. It can also give us access to experiences and opportunities that we may not have otherwise had. For example, we can travel to new places, try new hobbies, and meet new people.

However, research has shown that once our basic needs are met, additional money doesn't necessarily bring more happiness. Studies have found that people who prioritize money and material possessions tend to be less happy than those who prioritize experiences and relationships.

This is because money can't buy the things that truly bring us happiness. It can't buy love, friendship, or a sense of purpose. It can't buy good health or inner peace. These things come from within and are not dependent on external factors like money.

Furthermore, the pursuit of money can detract from our happiness. It can lead to stress, anxiety, and a constant sense of striving for more. It can also cause us to neglect other important areas of our lives like our relationships, our health, and our personal growth.

So, while money does play a role in our happiness, it's important to put it in perspective. We should strive to have enough money to meet our basic needs and pursue our passions, but we should not make it the sole focus of our lives. Instead, we should prioritize experiences, relationships, and personal growth as the true sources of happiness.

By understanding the connection between money and happiness, we can create a more balanced and fulfilling life. We can enjoy the benefits of financial stability while also cultivating the things that truly bring us joy and fulfillment.

Strategies for achieving financial stability and success

Achieving financial stability and success is a vital component of a happy and fulfilling life. Financial stability provides a sense of security and peace of mind, allowing us to focus on our other life goals without worrying about our finances. Here are some strategies to help you achieve financial stability and success.

1. Set clear financial goals: When it comes to achieving financial stability, it's essential to set clear financial goals. Be specific about what you want to achieve financially, whether it's paying off debt, saving for a down payment on a house, or investing in your retirement. Setting clear financial goals will help you stay motivated and focused on achieving your objectives.

2. Create a budget: Creating a budget is an essential step in achieving financial stability. A budget will help you keep track of your income and expenses, and identify areas where you can cut back on your spending. Make sure you prioritize your expenses, such as rent or mortgage, utilities, groceries, and transportation. By creating a budget, you'll be able to manage your money better and avoid overspending.

3. Manage your debt: If you have debt, it's essential to manage it effectively. Make sure you pay off high-interest debts first, such as credit card debt, and prioritize your debt payments in your budget. Consider consolidating your debt into a single payment to make it more manageable.

4. Save for emergencies: Unexpected expenses can happen at any time, which is why it's essential to have an emergency fund. Aim to save at least three to six months' worth of living expenses in your emergency fund. This will give you peace of mind and ensure that you're prepared for any unforeseen circumstances.

5. Invest in your future: Investing in your future is an important step in achieving financial stability and success. Consider investing in a retirement account, such as a 401(k) or IRA. Investing in stocks and other financial instruments can also be a good way to grow your wealth over time.

By following these strategies, you can achieve financial stability and success, which will bring you closer to a happy and fulfilling life. Remember that achieving financial stability takes time and effort, but the rewards are worth it.

The impact of financial security on happiness

Financial security is a crucial aspect of our overall well-being, and it is directly linked to our happiness. Research has shown that people who feel financially secure tend to be happier than those who don't. Financial stability provides us with a sense of security, which can help us feel more content and at peace with our lives.

One of the most significant impacts of financial security on happiness is the reduction of stress. Financial stress is one of the most common stressors in our lives. The worry and anxiety that come with financial insecurity can be overwhelming and can take a toll on our mental health. When we are financially secure, we can focus on other areas of our lives, such as our relationships, careers, and personal growth, without constantly worrying about money.

Furthermore, financial security can help us achieve our goals and dreams. When we have a stable income and savings, we can invest in our future and work towards our long-term aspirations. This can include buying a home, starting a business, or traveling the world. Financial security provides us with the means to pursue our passions and live the life we want, which can greatly contribute to our overall happiness.

Financial stability also plays a significant role in our relationships. Money issues are one of the leading causes of stress and conflict in relationships. When we are financially secure, we can avoid the tension and disagreements that arise from financial insecurity. Moreover, financial stability can allow us to support our loved ones and contribute to their happiness, which can strengthen our relationships and bring us closer together.

In conclusion, financial security is a vital component of our happiness and well-being. It provides us with a sense of security, reduces stress, helps us achieve our goals, and enhances our relationships. By prioritizing our financial stability, we can create a foundation for a more joyful and fulfilling life.

CHAPTER 8: HAPPINESS THROUGH PERSONAL GROWTH AND DEVELOPMENT

The importance of personal growth in finding happiness

The pursuit of happiness is a universal goal shared by all individuals. Yet, despite our best efforts to attain happiness, it often eludes us. This is because happiness is not something that can be bought or acquired through external means, but rather, it is something that must be cultivated from within. And the key to cultivating happiness lies in personal growth and development.

Personal growth is the process of self-discovery and self-improvement. It involves expanding our knowledge, skills, and abilities, and exploring our inner selves to uncover our true potentials. Personal growth is essential for finding happiness because it helps us to build a strong sense of self, develop a positive outlook on life, and increase our capacity for resilience and adaptability.

In the workplace, personal growth is crucial for career advancement and job satisfaction. It enables us to learn new skills, take on new challenges, and develop a growth mindset that allows us to thrive in a constantly changing work environment. Personal growth also plays a vital role in fostering healthy and fulfilling relationships. By becoming more self-aware and emotionally intelligent, we are better equipped to communicate effectively, resolve conflicts, and build deeper connections with our loved ones.

Physical fitness and wellness are also integral components of personal growth. By taking care of our bodies, we can improve our mental and emotional well-being, boost our self-confidence, and increase our energy levels. Engaging in creative pursuits and self-expression is another powerful way to promote personal growth and happiness. When we express ourselves through art, music, writing, or other forms of creative expression, we tap into our innermost thoughts and feelings and gain a deeper understanding of ourselves and the world around us.

Spirituality and mindfulness are also essential for personal growth and happiness. By cultivating a sense of inner peace and connection with something greater than ourselves, we can find meaning and purpose in our lives, and develop a greater sense of empathy and compassion towards others. And of course, financial stability and success are crucial for personal growth and happiness. When we can provide for ourselves and our loved ones, we feel a sense of security and fulfillment that allows us to pursue our passions and live life to the fullest.

In conclusion, personal growth is an essential component of finding happiness in all areas of life. By embracing personal growth and development, we can unlock our true potential, cultivate a positive outlook on life, and build fulfilling relationships, careers, and lives. So, let's commit ourselves to the joyful path of personal growth and discover the happiness that lies within us all.

Strategies for self-discovery and personal development

Self-discovery is a journey that requires time, effort, and a willingness to be vulnerable. The process of learning about ourselves can be both exciting and challenging, but the rewards of personal growth and development are immeasurable. In this chapter, we will explore some strategies for self-discovery and personal development that can help you find happiness and fulfillment in various aspects of your life.

1. Mindfulness and Meditation

Mindfulness and meditation are practices that can help you develop a deeper understanding of yourself. These practices involve focusing your attention on the present moment and observing your thoughts and emotions without judgment. By practicing mindfulness and meditation, you can learn to recognize patterns in your thinking and behavior and gain insight into your inner world.

2. Journaling

Journaling is a powerful tool for self-discovery and personal growth. Writing down your thoughts and feelings can help you process your emotions, gain clarity about your values and goals, and identify areas for improvement. Set aside time each day to write in a journal, and be honest and reflective in your writing.

3. Self-Care

Self-care is an essential aspect of self-discovery and personal growth. Taking care of your physical, emotional, and mental health can help you feel more balanced and resilient. Establish self-care routines that work for you, such as exercising regularly, eating healthy foods, getting enough sleep, and engaging in activities that bring you joy.

4. Learning and Growth

Learning new skills and knowledge can help you expand your perspective and develop new abilities. Take courses, read books, attend workshops, or listen to podcasts on topics that interest you. Learning can also help you build confidence and increase your sense of self-worth.

5. Seeking Support

Seeking support from others can be an important part of self-discovery and personal growth. Talk to trusted friends or family members, or seek the guidance of a professional therapist or coach. Sharing your thoughts and feelings with others can help you gain perspective and find new ways of approaching challenges.

In conclusion, self-discovery and personal development are ongoing processes that require intention and effort. By practicing mindfulness, journaling, self-care, learning and growth, and seeking support, you can gain valuable insights into yourself and find greater happiness and fulfillment in all aspects of your life.

The impact of personal growth on happiness and fulfillment

Personal growth is an essential aspect of leading a fulfilling life. When we actively seek to better ourselves, we tap into our full potential and discover new ways to experience happiness and contentment.

One of the significant impacts of personal growth is the increased sense of self-awareness and self-confidence. When we take the time to reflect on our thoughts, emotions, and behaviors, we become more attuned to our needs and desires. This self-awareness allows us to make better decisions that align with our values and goals, leading to a greater sense of fulfillment.

Personal growth also encourages us to step outside of our comfort zones and take on new challenges. When we push ourselves to try new things and take risks, we grow and develop in ways we never thought possible. These experiences can be incredibly empowering and boost our self-esteem, leading to increased happiness and satisfaction.

In the workplace, personal growth can lead to increased job satisfaction and career advancement. When we actively seek to develop new skills and knowledge, we become more valuable employees and are more likely to be considered for promotions and other opportunities. This sense of achievement can lead to increased happiness and motivation, both in our professional and personal lives.

In relationships, personal growth can lead to improved communication and deeper connections. When we are self-aware and confident in ourselves, we are better equipped to express our needs and emotions healthily. This can lead to more fulfilling, meaningful relationships with those around us.

Personal growth can also lead to improved physical and mental well-being. When we prioritize our health and wellness, we can experience increased energy, better sleep, and reduced stress and anxiety. This can have a significant impact on our overall happiness and quality of life.

Ultimately, personal growth is a lifelong journey that can lead to increased happiness and fulfillment in all aspects of our lives. By actively seeking to better ourselves and tap into our full potential, we can experience a greater sense of purpose and joy in our lives.

CHAPTER 9: HAPPINESS IN PARENTHOOD AND FAMILY LIFE

The impact of family and parenting on happiness

Family and parenting play a vital role in shaping an individual's happiness. The significance of family and parenting in the pursuit of happiness cannot be overstated. Research shows that people who have strong family ties and healthy relationships with their parents tend to be happier than those who don't.

One of the primary ways that family and parenting affect our happiness is through the support and love that we receive from them. Having a supportive family and parents who love and care for us unconditionally can provide us with a sense of security and comfort that can boost our overall happiness levels.

Another way that family and parenting can impact our happiness is through the values and beliefs that they instill in us. Our parents and family members are often our first teachers, and they play a significant role in shaping our worldview and moral code. If we are raised with positive values and beliefs, then we are more likely to experience happiness and fulfillment in our lives.

Additionally, the quality of our relationships with our family members and parents can have a significant impact on our overall happiness. Healthy, positive relationships can provide us with a sense of belonging and connection that can enhance our well-being.

However, it's important to note that family and parenting can also have negative effects on our happiness if we experience dysfunction or conflict within these relationships. Toxic family dynamics or abusive parenting can lead to feelings of unhappiness and trauma.

In conclusion, the impact of family and parenting on happiness is significant. If we are fortunate enough to have healthy, supportive relationships with our family members and parents, then we are more likely to experience happiness and fulfillment in our lives. However, it's important to recognize that not everyone has positive experiences with family and parenting, and it's essential to seek out support and resources if we are struggling with these relationships.

Strategies for finding happiness as a parent or family member

Parenthood and family life can be an incredible source of joy, but it can also be incredibly challenging at times. As a parent or family member, it's important to prioritize your happiness so that you can show up as your best self for your loved ones. Here are some strategies for finding happiness amid the chaos of parenthood and family life.

1. Focus on the present moment

It's easy to get caught up in worrying about the future or ruminating on the past, but this can lead to anxiety and stress. Instead, try to focus on the present moment as much as possible. Practice mindfulness by paying attention to your breath, your senses, and your surroundings. This can help you feel more grounded and centered, even amid a busy day.

2. Cultivate gratitude

Gratitude is a powerful tool for cultivating happiness. Take time each day to reflect on what you're grateful for, whether it's your family, your health, your home, or something else. You can do this through journaling, prayer, or simply taking a few minutes to think about what you appreciate in your life.

3. Set boundaries

As a parent or family member, it's important to set boundaries to protect your own well-being. This might mean saying no to commitments that don't align with your values or priorities, or setting limits on screen time or other activities that drain your energy. When you prioritize your own needs, you'll have more energy and enthusiasm to give to your loved ones.

4. Find joy in the small moments

Happiness doesn't have to come from big, dramatic events. Often, it's the small moments of joy that add up to a fulfilling life. Take time to savor a cup of coffee, play with your kids, or enjoy a good book. These moments of joy can help you feel more connected to your family and more content in your daily life.

5. Practice self-care

Self-care is essential for happiness, especially amid the demands of parenthood and family life. Make time for activities that nourish your body, mind, and soul, whether it's exercise, meditation, creative pursuits, or simply taking a relaxing bath. When you prioritize your well-being, you'll be better equipped to handle the challenges of family life with grace and resilience.

By following these strategies, you can find greater happiness and fulfillment as a parent or family member. Remember, your happiness is an essential ingredient in creating a happy, healthy family.

The impact of healthy family dynamics on happiness

The impact of healthy family dynamics on happiness is immense. A healthy family is a key ingredient to a happy life. Family dynamics are how family members interact with each other. It includes communication patterns, roles and responsibilities, and the emotional climate within the family. When these dynamics are healthy, it can have a positive impact on an individual's happiness.

First and foremost, a healthy family provides a sense of belonging and support. Knowing that you have a family that loves and cares for you unconditionally can give you a sense of security and self-worth. When family members feel supported and loved, they are more likely to experience happiness.

A healthy family also promotes effective communication. Communication is key in any relationship, and the same applies to family dynamics. When family members communicate effectively, they can resolve conflicts, express their needs and opinions, and build stronger relationships. This leads to a more harmonious family environment, which can contribute to happiness.

Furthermore, healthy family dynamics encourage personal growth and development. When family members support and encourage each other's goals and aspirations, individuals are more likely to achieve their full potential. This can lead to a sense of accomplishment and satisfaction, which can contribute to overall happiness.

In addition to personal growth, healthy family dynamics can also lead to a greater sense of empathy and compassion. When family members can understand and relate to each other's feelings and experiences, they are more likely to show kindness and support.

Overall, the impact of healthy family dynamics on happiness cannot be overstated. The benefits of a healthy family extend beyond just personal happiness but also contribute to happiness in other areas of life such as work, relationships, and personal growth. Therefore, it is important to prioritize and cultivate healthy family dynamics to experience a happy and fulfilling life.

CHAPTER 10: HAPPINESS IN TRAVEL AND EXPLORATION

The connection between travel and happiness

The connection between travel and happiness is undeniable. When we travel, we step out of our comfort zone, experience new cultures, and broaden our perspectives. It's no wonder that travel is often associated with joy, adventure, and self-discovery.

Happiness in Travel and Exploration

Traveling allows us to break free from our daily routines and explore the world around us. Whether it's visiting a new city, trying new foods, or meeting new people, travel opens the door to new experiences that can bring us happiness.

For many people, travel is a way to escape the stresses of everyday life. When we travel, we leave behind our work, responsibilities, and worries and focus on enjoying the present moment. This can be incredibly liberating and fulfilling.

Happiness Through Personal Growth and Development

Travel also offers opportunities for personal growth and development. When we travel, we are exposed to new ideas, ways of thinking, and ways of living. This exposure can help us develop a greater sense of empathy, compassion, and understanding for others.

Travel can also help us develop new skills and talents. For example, learning a new language or trying a new activity while on vacation can help us build confidence and self-esteem.

Happiness in Relationships

Traveling with loved ones can also bring us happiness and strengthen our relationships. When we travel with others, we create shared memories and experiences that can deepen our bonds. Whether it's a romantic getaway or a family vacation, travel can help us connect with others in meaningful ways.

Happiness Through Financial Stability and Success

While travel can be expensive, it doesn't have to break the bank. With careful planning and budgeting, travel can be an affordable and rewarding experience. And those who prioritize travel as a source of happiness, financial success, and stability can be a means to achieving their travel goals.

In conclusion, travel is a powerful source of happiness and self-discovery. Whether it's exploring a new city, trying new foods, or meeting new people, travel offers endless opportunities for growth and joy. By prioritizing travel in our lives, we can cultivate greater happiness and fulfillment.

Strategies for incorporating travel and exploration into life

Travel and exploration are some of the most exciting and enriching experiences that life has to offer. They allow us to broaden our horizons, discover new cultures and perspectives, and create lasting memories that we can treasure for a lifetime. However, many people struggle to incorporate travel and exploration into their lives due to various circumstances such as financial constraints, limited time, or a lack of motivation.

If you're one of those people, don't worry. There are many strategies that you can use to make travel and exploration a regular part of your life, regardless of your circumstances. Here are some tips to help you get started:

1. Start small

You don't have to travel to a far-off land to experience the joys of travel and exploration. Start by exploring your city or town. Visit local museums, art galleries, and historical landmarks. Attend cultural festivals and events. You may be surprised at how much there is to discover in your backyard.

2. Plan ahead

If you're serious about traveling and exploring, it's important to plan. Set realistic goals and start saving money for your next adventure. Research your destination and create a detailed itinerary. This will help you make the most of your time and ensure that you don't miss out on any must-see attractions.

3. Embrace spontaneity

While planning is important, don't be afraid to embrace spontaneity. Sometimes the best trips are the ones that are unplanned and spontaneous. Be open to new experiences and opportunities and don't be afraid to step outside your comfort zone.

4. Travel with purpose

Traveling with purpose can make your trips more meaningful and fulfilling. Consider volunteering abroad, learning a new skill, or taking part in a cultural exchange program. These experiences can help you connect with the local community, gain new perspectives, and make a positive impact.

5. Take advantage of technology

Technology has made travel and exploration easier than ever before. Use travel apps and websites to find the best deals on flights, accommodations, and activities. Use social media to connect with locals and other travelers and get insider tips on the best places to visit.

Incorporating travel and exploration into your life can lead to a happier, more fulfilling life. Whether you're exploring your city or traveling to a far-off destination, the key is to be open to new experiences, embrace spontaneity, and travel with purpose. So start planning your next adventure today and see where the joyful path takes you.

The impact of new experiences on happiness

The impact of new experiences on happiness is an important topic that needs to be explored. As humans, we tend to get comfortable with what we know, but sometimes we forget that life is full of surprises and new experiences. These experiences can have a significant impact on our happiness and overall well-being.

When we try something new, it can be scary, but it can also be exhilarating. Our brains release dopamine, a chemical associated with pleasure when we experience something new. This rush of dopamine can lead to an increase in happiness and an overall sense of well-being. Whether it's trying a new hobby, exploring a new place, or meeting new people, new experiences can help us feel more alive and connected to the world around us.

New experiences can also help us grow and develop as individuals. When we challenge ourselves to try something new, we are expanding our comfort zones and pushing ourselves to be better. This can lead to increased confidence and self-esteem, which are important components of happiness.

In the workplace, trying new things can help us feel more engaged and motivated. When we are stuck in a routine, we can become bored and disengaged from our work. Trying new projects or taking on new responsibilities can help us feel more fulfilled and satisfied with our jobs.

In relationships, trying new things together can help us feel more connected to our partners. Trying new activities or exploring new places can create shared experiences and memories that strengthen our relationships.

In fitness and wellness, trying new activities can help us find new ways to stay active and healthy. It can also help us break through fitness plateaus and avoid boredom in our workouts.

In creativity and self-expression, trying new forms of expression can help us tap into our creative potential and find new ways to express ourselves.

In spirituality and mindfulness, trying new practices or exploring different belief systems can help us deepen our understanding of ourselves and the world around us.

In financial stability and success, trying new ways to manage our finances or exploring new career opportunities can help us feel more in control of our lives and more fulfilled in our work.

In personal growth and development, trying new challenges can help us discover our strengths and weaknesses and push ourselves to be better.

In parenthood and family life, trying new family activities or exploring new ways to connect with our children can help us create stronger bonds and happier relationships.

In travel and exploration, trying new destinations or exploring new cultures can help us gain a broader perspective on the world and open our minds to new possibilities.

In community involvement and social activism, trying new ways to get involved in our communities or exploring new ways to make a difference can help us feel more connected to the world around us and more fulfilled in our contributions.

Overall, trying new things can have a powerful impact on our happiness and well-being. By stepping out of our comfort zones and embracing new experiences, we can lead richer, more fulfilling lives.

CHAPTER 11: HAPPINESS THROUGH COMMUNITY INVOLVEMENT AND SOCIAL ACTIVISM

The impact of community involvement and social activism on happiness

Community involvement and social activism can have a profound impact on an individual's happiness and sense of well-being. By engaging in activities that promote positive change in the world, we can find a deeper sense of purpose and fulfillment that goes beyond our personal needs and desires.

There are many different ways to get involved in your community and make a difference. Volunteering at a local charity or non-profit organization is a great way to give back and connect with others who share your values and passions. You might also consider joining a community group or activist organization that is working to promote social justice, environmental sustainability, or other important causes.

By becoming an active participant in your community, you can develop meaningful relationships with others and build a sense of belonging that is essential for happiness. When we feel connected to others and have a sense of purpose, we are more likely to experience positive emotions like joy, contentment, and fulfillment.

Social activism can also provide a sense of empowerment and agency that can boost our self-esteem and confidence.

When we take action to make a difference in the world, we feel like we are making a meaningful contribution and that our efforts matter. This can be especially important for individuals who may feel marginalized or powerless in other areas of their lives.

In addition to the personal benefits of community involvement and social activism, there are also many benefits for society as a whole. By working together to address social and environmental issues, we can create a more just and sustainable world that benefits everyone.

If you are looking for ways to increase your happiness and sense of purpose, consider getting involved in your community and becoming a social activist. Whether you volunteer at a local charity, join an activist organization, or simply start engaging more with your neighbors and community members, you can make a real difference in the world while also finding greater happiness and fulfillment in your own life.

Strategies for getting involved in community and social causes

Getting involved in community and social causes is an essential part of leading a fulfilling and happy life. It allows us to work towards the greater good, connect with others, and make a positive impact on the world. If you're interested in getting involved in community and social causes, here are some strategies that can help.

1. Identify your passion: Before you can get involved in community and social causes, you need to identify what issues are important to you. Think about what makes you angry, sad, or frustrated in the world and identify the causes that align with your values.

2. Research organizations: Once you've identified the causes that are important to you, it's time to research organizations that are working in those areas. Look for organizations that share your values and have a track record of success.

3. Volunteer your time: Volunteering is a great way to get involved and make a difference. Look for volunteer opportunities with organizations that align with your values and interests. Volunteering can also be a great way to meet like-minded people and build a sense of community.

4. Donate money: If you don't have the time to volunteer, consider donating money to organizations that are working on causes that are important to you. Even small donations can make a big difference.

5. Attend events: Attend events hosted by organizations that are working on causes that are important to you. This can be a great way to learn more about the cause, meet like-minded people, and build a sense of community.

6. Use your skills: Identify how your skills can be used to make a difference. For example, if you're a graphic designer, you could offer your services to create marketing materials for a nonprofit organization.

7. Start small: It's easy to get overwhelmed when you're trying to make a difference in the world. Start small by committing to volunteer once a month or donate a small amount of money each month. As you become more comfortable, you can increase your involvement.

Getting involved in community and social causes is an important part of leading a happy and fulfilling life. By identifying your passion, researching organizations, volunteering your time, donating money, attending events, using your skills, and starting small, you can make a positive impact on the world and build a sense of community.

The impact of giving back on happiness

Giving back to society has been proven to have a positive impact on one's happiness. The act of giving, whether it is through volunteering, donating money, or simply helping others, can give a sense of purpose and fulfillment that is hard to find in other areas of life.

Research has shown that people who engage in acts of kindness and generosity are more likely to experience positive emotions such as joy, gratitude, and contentment. These emotions, in turn, lead to an overall sense of happiness and well-being.

In the workplace, giving back can improve employee morale and satisfaction. When companies encourage their employees to participate in charitable activities, it creates a sense of community and purpose that can improve job satisfaction and reduce turnover rates.

In relationships, giving back can strengthen bonds and create a deeper sense of connection. Couples who volunteer together or support each other's charitable efforts often report feeling more connected and fulfilled in their relationships.

In terms of fitness and wellness, giving back can provide a sense of purpose and motivation to maintain a healthy lifestyle. For example, participating in a charity walk or run can give individuals a tangible goal to work towards while also benefiting a good cause.

In the realm of creativity and self-expression, giving back can provide a sense of purpose and meaning to artistic endeavors. For example, artists may choose to donate a portion of their profits to charity or create pieces that raise awareness for important social issues.

In spirituality and mindfulness, giving back can be seen as a form of service to others and an expression of compassion and empathy. Many spiritual traditions emphasize the importance of giving and service as a way to cultivate inner peace and happiness.

In terms of financial stability and success, giving back can provide a sense of purpose and meaning beyond material wealth. Many successful individuals choose to donate a portion of their wealth to charitable causes as a way to give back to society and create a positive impact.

In personal growth and development, giving back can provide a sense of purpose and direction. By engaging in charitable activities, individuals can develop new skills, meet new people, and gain a sense of fulfillment that can contribute to personal growth and development.

In parenthood and family life, giving back can teach

children important values such as compassion, empathy, and social responsibility. Families who volunteer together often report feeling closer and more connected as a result.

In travel and exploration, giving back can provide a unique and meaningful way to experience new cultures and communities. Many individuals choose to volunteer or donate to local organizations while traveling as a way to give back and make a positive impact.

In community involvement and social activism, giving back can be a powerful tool for creating positive change. By participating in local initiatives and supporting important social causes, individuals can contribute to a more just and equitable society while also experiencing a sense of purpose and fulfillment.

In summary, giving back has a significant impact on happiness across a wide range of areas. Whether it's in the workplace, relationships, fitness and wellness, creativity and self-expression, spirituality, and mindfulness, financial stability and success, personal growth and development, parenthood and family life, travel and exploration, or community involvement and social activism, giving back can provide a sense of purpose, fulfillment, and joy that is hard to find elsewhere.

CONCLUSION

Summary of key points

The Joyful Path: Finding Happiness Through Self-Discovery is a book that provides readers with insights and practical tips on how to find happiness and fulfillment in their lives. Throughout the book, readers are taken through a journey of self-discovery, learning about different aspects of themselves and the world around them.

In this subchapter, we will summarize the key points discussed in the book, highlighting the most important takeaways for readers.

One of the key messages of the book is that happiness is not something that can be achieved through external factors such as wealth, success, or material possessions. Rather, true happiness comes from within, and it is something that can be cultivated through self-discovery and personal growth.

The book discusses a range of different strategies and techniques that readers can use to enhance their happiness, including mindfulness, meditation, creative expression, physical activity, and community involvement. These strategies are designed to help readers connect with their inner selves and cultivate a sense of purpose and fulfillment in their lives.

Another important message of the book is that happiness is not a static state, but rather a dynamic and ever-changing process. This means that readers need to be willing to adapt and evolve, to maintain their sense of happiness and fulfillment.

Throughout the book, readers are encouraged to embrace their individuality and to celebrate their unique strengths and talents. By doing so, they can tap into their full potential and find greater meaning and happiness in their lives.

Overall, The Joyful Path is a powerful and inspiring book that offers readers a wealth of insights and practical tips on how to find happiness and fulfillment in their lives. Whether you are looking to improve your relationships, your career, your health, or your overall sense of well-being, this book has something to offer everyone. So why not start your journey of self-discovery today, and discover the joy that lies within you?

Final thoughts on finding happiness through self-discovery

As we come to the end of our journey towards finding happiness through self-discovery, it is important to reflect on the lessons we have learned and the progress we have made. Happiness is not a destination, but a journey that requires constant effort and self-awareness. It is a state of mind that can be cultivated through intentional actions and a commitment to personal growth and development.

In our pursuit of happiness, we must first acknowledge that it is not something that can be achieved through external factors such as wealth, success, or relationships. While these things may bring temporary pleasure, true happiness comes from within and is rooted in self-awareness, self-acceptance, and self-love.

One of the key lessons we have learned is the importance of mindfulness in our daily lives. By practicing mindfulness, we can stay present in the moment, appreciate the beauty around us, and cultivate a sense of gratitude for what we have. This helps us to overcome negative thoughts and emotions and find joy in even the simplest of things.

We have also learned that happiness is not a one-size-fits-all concept and that what brings joy to one person may not be the same for another. It is important to explore our interests, passions, and values and align our lives accordingly. This may mean pursuing a career that brings us fulfillment or engaging in creative activities that allow us to express ourselves.

Financial stability is also an important factor in our pursuit of happiness. While money cannot buy happiness, it can provide us with a sense of security and freedom that allows us to pursue our passions and live the life we desire.

In conclusion, finding happiness through self-discovery is a journey that requires ongoing effort and self-reflection. By cultivating mindfulness, exploring our passions and values, and aligning our lives accordingly, we can create a fulfilling and joyful life. Remember, happiness is not a destination, but a state of mind that can be cultivated through intentional actions and a commitment to personal growth and development.

ABOUT THE AUTHOR

Sales and Marketing Professional with more than 25 Plus years of diversified experience for both transnational and national pharmaceutical companies such as Merck & Co. Inc. NV Organon, AkzoNobel, and OBS Pakistan (Pvt.) Limited. Moreover, he is a university Professor and has more than 10 years' experience of teaching, research and supervising dissertations for MBA, MS. M.Phil., and Ph.D. level students. He is an author and coauthor of more than 200 publications, in which he has written more than 80 impact factor research articles, and 20 books.